EDUCATION 5.0: PREPARING FOR AN UNPREDICTABLE FUTURE

DR DHEERAJ MEHROTRA

Contents

Preface   *v*

  1. Introduction To Education 5.0   1

  2. Understanding Education 5.0   7

  3. Personalized Learning In Education 5.0   18

  4. Collaboration: Learning Through Teamwork   24

  5. Well-being: The Emotional Core Of Learning   29

  6. Industry Relevance: Bridging Education And Future Careers   35

  7. Skill Development For The 21st Century   41

  8. Technological Tools And Methods In Education 5.0   47

  9. Implementing Education 5.0   61

10. Case Studies And Success Stories   71

11. Future Of Education 5.0   76

12. 25 Paths To Implementing Education 5.0   82

13. 10 "Do-Nots" For The Implementation Of Education 5.0 In   86
    Schools

About The Author   91

Books By The Same Author   93

References: Further Reading   95

Preface

Education is the cornerstone of progress, and in today's fast-evolving world, it must adapt to prepare learners for unprecedented challenges and opportunities. As we enter an era of rapid technological advancements, global connectivity, and complex societal changes, traditional education methods are no longer sufficient. This realization forms the foundation of Education 5.0, a transformative approach designed to empower students as lifelong learners, innovators, and socially responsible citizens.

*This book, **Education 5.0: Preparing for an Unpredictable Future**, explores the critical need for a paradigm shift in education. It delves into the core principles of personalized learning, collaboration, emotional well-being, industry relevance, and skill development that underpin this new model. By integrating technology and fostering adaptability, Education 5.0 aims to equip students with the tools they need to thrive in a world where the only constant is change.*

This book combines strategies with real-world examples. It is intended for educators, policymakers, and stakeholders committed to revolutionizing education. Each chapter unpacks the key elements of Education 5.0, offering insights into its implementation and potential impact on learners and society.

As you embark on this journey, I invite you to imagine the possibilities of an education system that imparts knowledge and nurtures creativity, resilience, and empathy. Together, let us embrace the challenge of preparing the next generation for a future brimming with uncertainty and opportunity.

Author

www.authordheerajmehrotra.com

ONE

Introduction to Education 5.0

"Education 5.0 is not just about learning how to use technology
but about creating mindful, empathetic, and globally aware
citizens using technology as a tool."
– Dr. Tony Wagner, Education Specialist

Introduction to Education 5.0

*Education 5.0 is a revolutionary learning paradigm
that amalgamates cutting-edge technology with*

humanistic principles, emphasising personalised, competency-driven, and experiential education. It underscores creativity, critical thinking, cooperation, and problem-solving to equip pupils for the difficulties of a swiftly changing world. Education 5.0 in schools emphasises the incorporation of AI, AR/VR, and digital technologies to enhance engagement and tailor learning to individual needs. It advocates for a comprehensive development paradigm that integrates academic proficiency with emotional intelligence and ethical consciousness, ensuring students are prepared for the workforce and empowered global citizens capable of effecting significant change.

Conventional Educational Approaches

Conventional education has historically been defined by a teacher-centred model, wherein knowledge is predominantly conveyed from educator to learner. This paradigm frequently prioritises rote memorisation and standardised assessments, concentrating on acquiring information rather than critical thinking or problem-solving abilities. Although applicable in specific situations, this strategy has been criticised for its failure to adapt to the swiftly evolving demands of the contemporary world.

Factors Influencing the Transition

A multitude of crucial elements has facilitated the transition to more modern educational paradigms:

Technological Advancements: The emergence of digital technology has revolutionised information access and dissemination methods. Digital learning platforms, educational applications, and interactive resources have enhanced accessibility and engagement in education.

Globalisation: As the world becomes more interconnected, educational systems must increasingly educate students for a global workforce. This needs a curriculum that prioritises cultural awareness and cooperation.

Shifting Workforce Requirements: Employers pursue candidates with competencies beyond conventional academic expertise. Critical thinking, inventiveness, and adaptability have become crucial skills in the employment sector.

Student-Centered Learning: The significance of tailored learning experiences that address individual student requirements, interests, and learning preferences is increasingly acknowledged.

What is new in Education 5.0?

Education 5.0 signifies a transformative transformation to amalgamate technology, human values, and novel teaching methodologies. This paradigm underscores the necessity of equipping students for particular professions and continuous learning and flexibility in a constantly changing environment. The fundamental principle of Education 5.0 revolves around:

Comprehensive Development: Cultivating emotional, social, and cognitive competencies to produce well-rounded persons.

Interdisciplinary Learning: Promoting collaboration among diverse disciplines to address intricate issues.

Practical Application: Integrating classroom instruction with real-world difficulties to augment relevance and engagement.

"Education 5.0 is not just about adapting to technology; it's about ensuring that technology adapts to humanity's needs and values."
– Prof. Anil Sahasrabudhe, AICTE Chairman

The transition from traditional educational techniques to Education 5.0 signifies a significant transformation in our comprehension of teaching and learning. By adopting innovative technologies and instructional methods, we may more effectively prepare students for future uncertainties, providing them with the skills and mentality essential for success in a dynamic environment.

❧❧❧

TWO

UNDERSTANDING EDUCATION 5.0

"In Education 5.0, the classroom transforms into a collaborative space where AI and human intelligence unite to build a sustainable future."
– Sir Ken Robinson, Education Innovator

Understanding Education 5.0

Education 5.0 is a transformational teaching approach that uses technology to prepare students for a rapidly changing environment. This unique educational paradigm prioritises the creation of lifelong learners capable of navigating new difficulties and devising solutions that benefit society. Education 5.0 seeks to prepare students for an uncertain future by combining personalised learning, teamwork, emotional well-being, industrial relevance, and necessary skill development.

Features of Education 5.0

Personalised Learning

Education 5.0 employs advanced digital tools such as Artificial Intelligence (AI), Virtual Reality (VR), and the Internet of Things (IoT) to create personalised learning experiences suited to each student's specific requirements and preferences. This personalised approach allows learners to proceed at their own pace and connect with content that speaks to them.

Collaboration

This educational paradigm promotes a collaborative environment in which students work together to solve complex challenges and develop new solutions. Education 5.0 promotes cooperation, allowing students to develop critical interpersonal skills and learn from various perspectives.

Well-being

Education 5.0 emphasises pupils' emotional and social development. It prioritises abilities such as empathy, creativity, and resilience, ensuring that students are academically successful and prepared to address the emotional challenges of today's world.

Industry Relevance

In a landscape where many occupations have yet to be established, Education 5.0 educates students for future careers that do not yet exist. By connecting educational goals with industry needs, this model prepares students to prosper in developing fields and adapt to changing labour markets.

Skill Development

Education 5.0 focuses on 21st-century skills such as critical thinking, creativity, and problem-solving. These qualities are required for students to negotiate the intricacies of modern life and make meaningful contributions to their communities.

How Does Education 5.0 Work?

Education 5.0 modernises existing teaching methods by establishing student-centred learning environments. Educators use technology to promote active learning, allowing students to apply their knowledge in real-world settings. Problem-based and research-based activities empower learners to produce new information, building a more profound comprehension of their study subjects.

Components of Education 5.0

Education 5.0 prepares students for the challenges of the modern world by integrating advanced technology, human-centric learning, and holistic development. The primary components are as follows:

1. Customised Education

What it Means: Educational experiences that are customised to meet the unique needs, interests, and capabilities of each student.

Tools: Real-time feedback systems, adaptive assessments, and AI-driven learning platforms.

2. Competency-Based Education

What it Means: Emphasise the acquisition of knowledge and skills over time-based advancement.

Advantages: Guarantees that students acquire the fundamental skills required for both their personal and professional lives.

3. Introduction of Artificial Intelligence into the Learning

What it Means: The utilisation of artificial intelligence for the purpose of content recommendation, assessment, and personalised tutoring.

For instance, predictive analytics, intelligent tutoring systems, and chatbots powered by AI.

4. Immersive and Experiential Learning

What it Means: Interactive and practical learning experiences that utilise AR/VR.

Applications: Historical recreations, virtual field excursions, and laboratory simulations.

5. STEAM Emphasis

Integrated learning is achieved by integrating science, technology, engineering, arts, and mathematics.

Objective: Fosters critical thinking and problem-solving in conjunction with creativity.

6. Cultural and Global Awareness

What it Means: Providing students with an understanding of cultural diversity and global issues.

Activities: Cross-cultural exchanges and global collaboration initiatives.

7. Emotional Intelligence and Ethics

What it Means: Instructing students on the concepts of social responsibility, emotional awareness, and empathy.

Focus: The cultivation of individuals who are well-rounded and possess strong moral principles.

8. Environmental Education and Sustainability

Definition: The promotion of sustainable practices and eco-consciousness in the educational environment.

Examples include community programs, climate education, and green campus initiatives.

9. Learning Enhanced by Technology

What it Means: Utilising cutting-edge technologies such as gamified learning systems, AR/VR, and IoT.

Results: Enhances the effectiveness, engagement, and interactivity of the learning process.

10. Problem-Solving and Critical Thinking

What it Means: Fostering students' ability to analyse, evaluate, and develop solutions.

Tools: Real-world challenges, project-based learning, and case studies.

11. Digital Citizenship and Literacy

What it Means: Educating students on the responsible and effective use of technology.

Content: The ethical use of data, online safety, and the navigation of digital environments.

12. Flexible and Hybrid Learning Models

What it Means: The integration of traditional and online learning methods to create a flexible learning experience.

Advantage: Offers learning opportunities that extend beyond the confines of the classroom.

13. Education that is driven by data

What it Means: Utilising analytics to monitor and enhance student performance.

Applications: Evidence-based teaching strategies, tailored curricula, and early interventions.

14. Emphasise Innovation and Creativity

What it Means: Fostering students' innovative and unconventional thinking.

Activities: Innovation challenges, design thinking workshops, and makerspaces.

15. Development of the Whole

What it Means: Maintaining a balance between academics, the arts, athletics, mental health, and life skills.

Objective: To cultivate pupils who are emotionally, physically, and intellectually well-rounded.

Education 5.0 is a forward-thinking strategy that prepares students for an uncertain future by emphasising personalised learning, collaboration, emotional well-being, industry relevance, and the development of critical skills. This educational approach will become increasingly important in developing adaptive, innovative, and socially responsible adults as we progress into the twenty-first century.

❧❧❧

THREE

PERSONALIZED LEARNING IN EDUCATION 5.0

"Learning in the Education 5.0 era means embracing adaptability and creativity as core skills, enabling students to shape a world we've yet to imagine."
– Dr. Sugata Mitra, Innovator in Digital Education

Education 5.0: Customised Instruction

The idea of personalised learning in education 5.0, which uses cutting-edge technologies like artificial intelligence (AI), virtual reality (VR), and the Internet of Things (IoT), stands out as a revolutionary strategy in the quickly changing field of education. This paper investigates how these technologies might be combined to give students individualised learning routes to improve their educational experience. It also covers the numerous advantages of personalised learning strategies, such as higher engagement and better academic results.

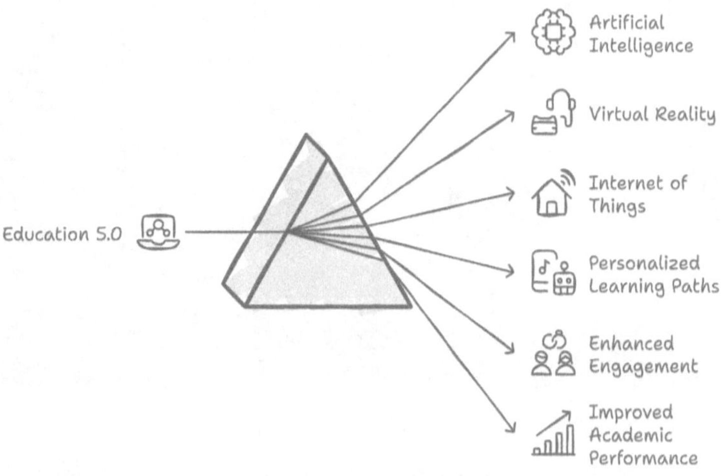

AI's Place in Tailored Education

Artificial intelligence is heavily relied upon to create customised learning environments. By analysing large volumes of data on academic achievement, AI can identify each student's unique learning preferences, talents, and shortcomings. Teachers may use this data to tailor their courses and provide materials aligned with each student's needs. AI-powered systems can also adapt in real time, providing prompt assistance and feedback, thereby making learning more enjoyable.

Immersion Learning Experiences with Virtual Reality

Immersion learning experiences enabled by virtual reality technology have the potential to significantly increase student engagement. By simulating real-world situations, virtual reality enables students to investigate complex concepts in practice. For example, kids can perform science experiments in a secure setting or take virtual field tours to historical locations. In addition to making studying more engaging, this degree of interaction improves students' retention of knowledge.

The Internet of Things: Networked Educational Settings

The Internet of Things, which links various systems and devices, facilitates a seamless learning environment. IoT can support personalised learning in educational settings by enabling smart classrooms with sensors and devices that track student engagement and participation. Wearable technology, for instance, can monitor students' physiological responses, providing teachers with information about their emotional states and enabling them to modify their teaching methods accordingly. This connectedness promotes a more responsive and adaptable learning environment.

Advantages of Tailored Learning Strategies

There are several advantages of integrating AI, VR, and IoT into personalised learning:

Enhanced Involvement: Customised educational opportunities pique students' curiosity and inspire them to participate actively in their education.

Better Results: Personalised techniques have been demonstrated to enhance academic performance by attending to each student's unique learning demands and pace.

Increased Autonomy: Students have more excellent command over their educational trajectories, cultivating a sense of accountability and ownership.

Better Teacher-Student Relationships: Teachers who are more aware of each student's requirements can offer more significant support and direction

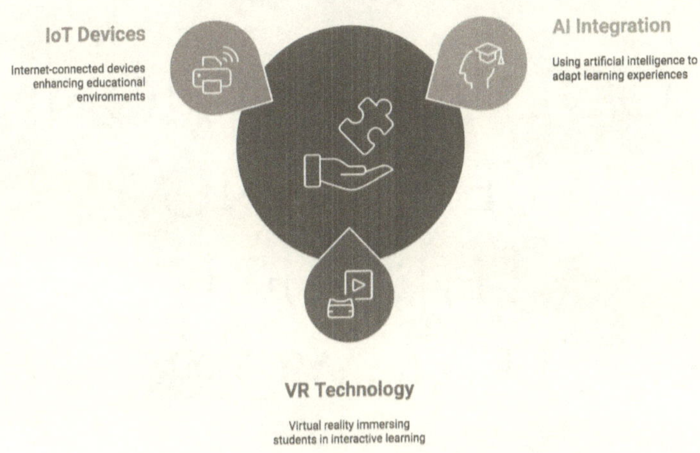

Personalised Learning in Education 5.0 represents a significant change in how education is provided and experienced. Teachers may use AI, VR, and IoT to design personalised learning pathways that meet their pupils' various needs. Such individualised techniques have significant advantages, including higher levels of engagement, better academic results, and a more satisfying educational experience. Adopting these technologies will be essential to determining how education develops in the future.

❧❧❧

FOUR

Collaboration: Learning Through Teamwork

"The power of Education 5.0 lies in its ability to blend
technology, ethics, and creativity, fostering not just skilled
professionals but empathetic problem-solvers."
– Dr. Anant Agarwal, CEO, edX

Collaboration: Acquiring Knowledge via Teamwork

*Collaboration is essential for tackling intricate issues
that require many skill sets and viewpoints. This
follows the importance of teamwork in promoting
practical cooperation, highlighting the cultivation of*

teamwork skills and the value of diverse perspectives. Understanding the dynamics of collaboration enables individuals to improve their problem-solving skills and foster more imaginative ideas.

The Significance of Collaboration

The capacity for effective collaboration is increasingly paramount in the contemporary interconnected world. Intricate difficulties frequently necessitate contributions from other disciplines, making it crucial to leverage the skills of a heterogeneous workforce. Collaboration facilitates the amalgamation of knowledge, skills, and experiences, resulting in more thorough and innovative solutions.

Developing Collaborative Competencies

To foster effective collaboration, individuals must develop key teamwork skills, including:

Communication: Transparent and direct communication is essential for exchanging ideas and feedback. Team members must feel comfortable articulating their opinions and concerns.

Active Listening: Attentive listening is equally vital as articulating one's thoughts. Active listening facilitates comprehension of diverse viewpoints among team members and cultivates a culture of respect.

Conflict Resolution: Disputes are inherent in any team environment. Enhancing conflict resolution abilities facilitates the constructive management of differences, which improves team dynamics.

Adaptability: Teams must be flexible and ready to modify their strategies as new facts and concepts emerge. Adaptability fosters resilience and inventiveness.

Cultivating Appreciation for Varied Perspectives

Diversity within teams provides a multitude of perspectives that can improve problem-solving capabilities. To foster an awareness of other perspectives, teams can:

Promote Inclusivity: Foster an environment where all team members are esteemed and embraced. This can be accomplished via team-building exercises and candid dialogues.

Honour Diversity: Recognise and appreciate team members' distinct backgrounds and experiences. This cultivates a sense of belonging and enhances the team's collective expertise.

Foster Empathy: Urge team members to consider each other's perspectives. Comprehending the experiences and perspectives of others helps facilitate more deliberate and inclusive decision-making.

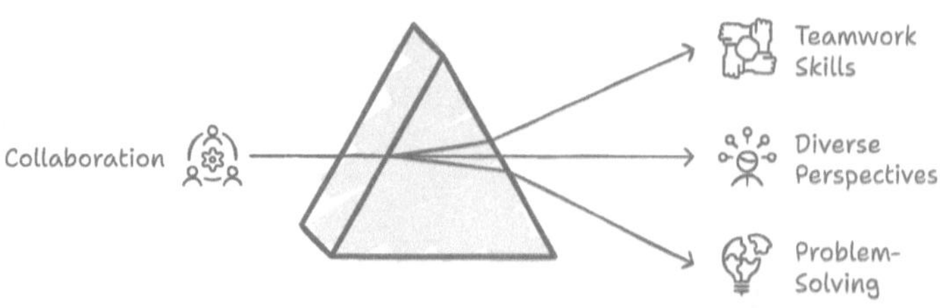

Collaboration is crucial for addressing intricate issues and fostering creativity. Individuals and teams can improve their joint endeavours by cultivating cooperation and promoting an appreciation for other viewpoints. Fostering collaboration yields superior solutions and cultivates a more inclusive and dynamic workplace.

FIVE

WELL-BEING: THE EMOTIONAL CORE OF LEARNING

"Education 5.0 places learners at the center of the ecosystem, encouraging personalized pathways to knowledge while equipping them to tackle real-world challenges."
– Dr. Andreas Schleicher, OECD Education Leader

The Significance of Emotional Well-being in Education

Emotional well-being is a fundamental component of education that affects cognitive processes, motivation, and overall academic achievement. Students who experience emotional security and support are more inclined to engage thoroughly with the topic, participate actively in conversations, and take chances in their learning. A deficiency in emotional backing can result in anxiety, disengagement, and impaired academic performance.

Methods for Instructing Empathy

Empathy is an essential trait that promotes connection and comprehension among students. Here are several excellent techniques to foster empathy in school environments:

Role-Playing Activities: Motivate students to assume different identities through role-playing scenarios emphasising varied viewpoints and experiences.

Literature and Storytelling: Use texts and narratives that examine intricate emotional issues, facilitating dialogue about characters' emotions and motivations.

Community Service Initiatives: Engage students in community service to facilitate interaction with varied groups and enhance their understanding of varying life circumstances.

Fostering Resilience

Resilience is the capacity to recover from adversities and difficulties. Instructing resilience provides kids with the skills to manage challenges adeptly. Strategies encompass:

Growth Mindset Workshops: These workshops foster a growth mindset by instructing children that abilities can be cultivated through diligence and persistence.

Problem-Solving Exercises: Engage students with problems that necessitate critical thinking and innovative solutions, emphasising that failure is an integral aspect of the learning process.

Mindfulness Techniques: Implement mindfulness strategies to assist pupils in stress management and cultivating emotional regulation abilities.

Encouraging Innovation

Creativity is vital for innovation and issue resolution. Promoting creative thinking in the classroom can improve emotional well-being and academic achievement. Evaluate these methodologies:

Open-Ended Projects: Facilitate students' exploration of themes of interest via open-ended projects that promote self-expression and creativity.

Collaborative Learning: Encourage group work that enhances cooperation, allowing students to exchange ideas and augment one another's creativity.

Integration of Art and Music: Embed the arts and music throughout the curriculum to offer pupils diverse means for expression and emotional discovery.

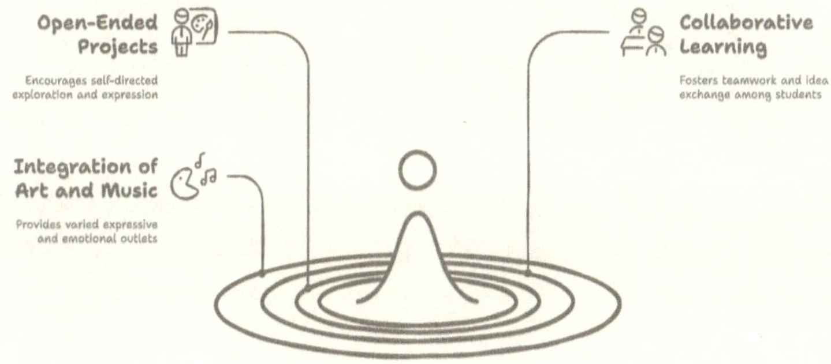

Emotional well-being constitutes the emotional foundation of learning and profoundly influences students' academic experiences. Educators may establish a more comprehensive educational environment that supports children's development by employing tactics that cultivate empathy, resilience, and creativity. Emphasising emotional well-being improves learning outcomes and equips pupils to succeed in a progressively intricate world.

ᗡᗡᗡ

SIX

INDUSTRY RELEVANCE: BRIDGING EDUCATION AND FUTURE CAREERS

"Education 5.0 is about nurturing humanity alongside innovation, teaching students not only how to create but how to create responsibly."
– Dr. Howard Gardner, Professor of Education at Harvard University

Industry Significance: Connecting Education and Prospective Careers

Education is crucial for meeting industrial requirements in a constantly changing employment market. This showcases the necessity of aligning educational curricula with the skills and abilities demanded by the workforce. It explores novel techniques for equipping students for future jobs that may not yet exist, highlighting the significance of adaptation and creativity in education.

The Evolving Employment Landscape

The swift progression of technology and globalisation has altered the job market, resulting in the rise of new industries and the decline of others. Consequently, conventional educational methods fail to give students the essential abilities to succeed in this evolving landscape. It is imperative to acknowledge that numerous future career opportunities are not yet in existence, requiring a transformation in our educational approach.

Encouraging Flexibility

To equip pupils for an unpredictable future, educational institutions must emphasise adaptability. This entails instructing students in particular skills and the processes of learning and unlearning in response to industry evolution. Integrating project-based learning, interdisciplinary studies, and real-world problem-solving into the curriculum fosters a mindset in students that encourages change and creativity.

Strategies for Improving Adaptability

Interdisciplinary Learning: Promote collaboration among diverse academic disciplines to build a comprehensive understanding of intricate issues.

Experiential Learning: Facilitate opportunities for students to participate in internships, cooperative education, and practical projects that reflect real-world challenges.

Perpetual Learning: Foster a culture of perpetual education, encouraging students to pursue knowledge and skills beyond traditional schooling.

Fostering Innovation

Innovation is a fundamental catalyst for economic expansion and employment generation. Educational institutions must provide an environment that promotes creativity and critical thinking. Integrating design thinking and entrepreneurial principles into the curriculum enables students to tackle challenges from a novel perspective and cultivate unique solutions.

Strategies for Fostering Innovation

Innovative Problem Resolution: Establish courses that emphasise brainstorming, prototyping, and evaluating concepts within a nurturing environment.

Industry Collaboration: Engage with enterprises to present students with practical difficulties necessitating inventive solutions.

Mentorship Programs: Facilitate connections between students and industry professionals who may motivate and direct them in their creative pursuits.

Connecting education with future employment is essential for equipping students to face the difficulties of the workforce ahead. Educational institutions can promote adaptation and creativity, equipping students with the necessary skills to thrive in a dynamic employment market. We must reevaluate our educational strategy to ensure its relevance and responsiveness to the demands of students and industry.

ᐅᐅᐅ

SEVEN

SKILL DEVELOPMENT FOR THE 21ST CENTURY

"In Education 5.0, we move beyond rote learning to foster a culture of curiosity and exploration, powered by AI and human ingenuity."
– Prof. Salman Khan, Founder of Khan Academy

Competency Advancement for the Twenty-First Century

In today's swiftly changing world, the need to provide pupils with fundamental skills is paramount. This document examines the essential abilities required for pupils to succeed in the 21ˢᵗ century, such as critical thinking, creativity, and problem-solving. It also examines how these talents can be effectively cultivated through active learning, ensuring that students are equipped to confront the difficulties of the contemporary workforce and society.

Fundamental Competencies for the 21ˢᵗ Century

Analytical Reasoning

Critical thinking encompasses the capacity to assess information, appraise evidence, and formulate rational conclusions. In an era characterised by an abundance of frequently deceptive information, cultivating critical thinking abilities is essential. Students must learn to interrogate preconceptions, recognise biases, and evaluate the credibility of sources. This ability allows them to address intricate issues and render informed choices.

Ingenuity

Creativity extends beyond creative expression; it is an essential skill that fosters innovation and facilitates problem-solving. In the 21ˢᵗ century, the capacity for innovative thinking and idea generation is crucial. Promoting creativity in students can result in creative solutions and progress across diverse disciplines. It facilitates their adaptation to change and encourages a receptive response to problems.

Issue Resolution

Problem-solving involves the capacity to recognise challenges, evaluate possible solutions, and execute effective techniques. This competence is essential in both academic and practical contexts. Students proficient in problem-solving can confront issues directly and cultivate resilience when faced with barriers. It involves synthesising critical thinking and creativity, establishing it as a fundamental component of 21st-century competencies.

Fostering Competencies via Engaged Learning

Active learning is an educational methodology that actively involves students in learning and promotes their accountability for their education. This approach is especially efficacious in cultivating the fundamental talents already mentioned.

Joint Endeavours

Collaborative endeavours and group assignments improve critical thinking and problem-solving abilities. Students are urged to exchange ideas, contest one another's viewpoints, and collaborate to identify answers. This collaborative setting deepens their comprehension of the material and equips students for future teamwork in their jobs.

Practical Engagements

Integrating experiential activities into the curriculum enables students to utilise their knowledge in practical contexts—experiments in science, design projects in art, and simulations in business foster creativity and critical thinking. Students get the skills to explore, iterate, and enhance their concepts, which is crucial for creativity.

Real-World Problem Solving

Involving students in practical issues enhances their understanding of the significance of their studies. Addressing challenges that affect their communities or the global environment cultivates a sense of purpose and accountability. This method improves students' problem-solving abilities and fosters critical thinking about their environment.

Contemplation and Evaluation

Promoting student reflection on their learning experiences and soliciting feedback is essential for improving their skills. Reflection facilitates comprehension of cognitive processes, identifies opportunities for improvement, and fosters self-awareness. Constructive feedback from colleagues and instructors further augments students' critical thinking and problem-solving skills.

In summary, critical thinking, creativity, and problem-solving skills are vital for pupils to succeed in the 21st century. Instructors can proficiently cultivate these talents by using active learning approaches, equipping students for the difficulties and possibilities that await. Our educational institutions must prioritise skill development to prepare future generations for success in a dynamic environment.

EIGHT

TECHNOLOGICAL TOOLS AND METHODS IN EDUCATION 5.0

"The essence of Education 5.0 is preparing students not just for jobs of today, but for careers that will emerge tomorrow."
– Dr. Eric Sheninger, Educational Leadership Specialist

Technological Instruments and Techniques in Education 5.0

Incorporating advanced tools such as gamification, virtual reality (VR) simulations, and artificial intelligence (AI)- driven tutors is transforming the dynamic educational landscape and fundamentally altering information dissemination and acquisition methods. The innovative technologies are converting traditional classrooms into dynamic, technology-enhanced learning environments, improving engagement, personalisation, and accessibility in education.

COMPONENTS OF EDUCATION 5.0

Augmented Reality (AR)

1. Contextual Learning

2. Hands-On Learning

3. Enhanced Visualization

Examples

(Google Expeditions AR, Aurasma, Quiver)

Gamification in Education

Gamification entails integrating game-like components into educational environments to enhance student engagement and motivation. By including points, badges, leaderboards, and challenges in the educational process, instructors may foster a more engaging and pleasurable experience. This method promotes constructive rivalry and cultivates a sense of accomplishment among pupils.

Platforms such as Kahoot! and Classcraft enable educators to create quizzes and exercises that resemble games rather than conventional assessments. This approach makes learning enjoyable and enhances students' retention of information, as they are more inclined to engage with content delivered engagingly.

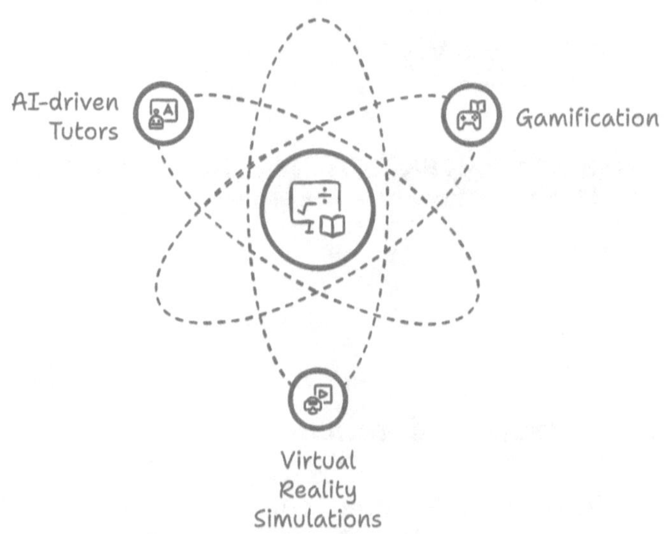

Simulations in Virtual Reality

Virtual reality (VR) simulations provide immersive experiences that can transport students to many places and circumstances, augmenting their comprehension of intricate ideas. In disciplines such as science, history, and geography, VR can offer students experiential learning opportunities unattainable in a conventional classroom environment.

COMPONENTS OF EDUCATION 5.0

Virtual Reality (VR)

1. Immersive Simulations

2. Experiential Learning

3. 3. Collaborative Learning

4. 4. Overcoming Physical Limitations

Examples

(Google Earth VR, Labster, AltspaceVR, Unimersiv)

Students can examine the human body in three

dimensions, explore ancient civilisations, or perform virtual chemistry experiments without the hazards associated with actual laboratory work. This practical method enhances understanding and accommodates diverse learning styles, fostering inclusivity in education.

Tutors Powered by Artificial Intelligence

Artificial intelligence transforms the educational landscape by delivering personalised learning experiences via AI-driven instructors. These clever technologies can evaluate individual student performance, pinpoint areas of difficulty, and customise instruction accordingly. This degree of customisation guarantees that each student obtains the necessary assistance for success.

COMPONENTS OF EDUCATION 5.0

Examples of Artificial Intelligence

1. Student Enrollment and Registration
2. Scheduling and Timetabling
3. Grading and Assessment
4. Attendance Tracking
5. Communication and Chatbots
6. Resource Allocation
7. Predictive Analytics for Student Retention

AI instructors, including Carnegie Learning and Squirrel AI, provide immediate feedback, recommend further resources, and adjust to the learner's pace. This technology improves student comprehension and enables educators to concentrate on more intricate educational responsibilities since they can depend on AI to manage routine evaluations and feedback.

General Learning Platforms

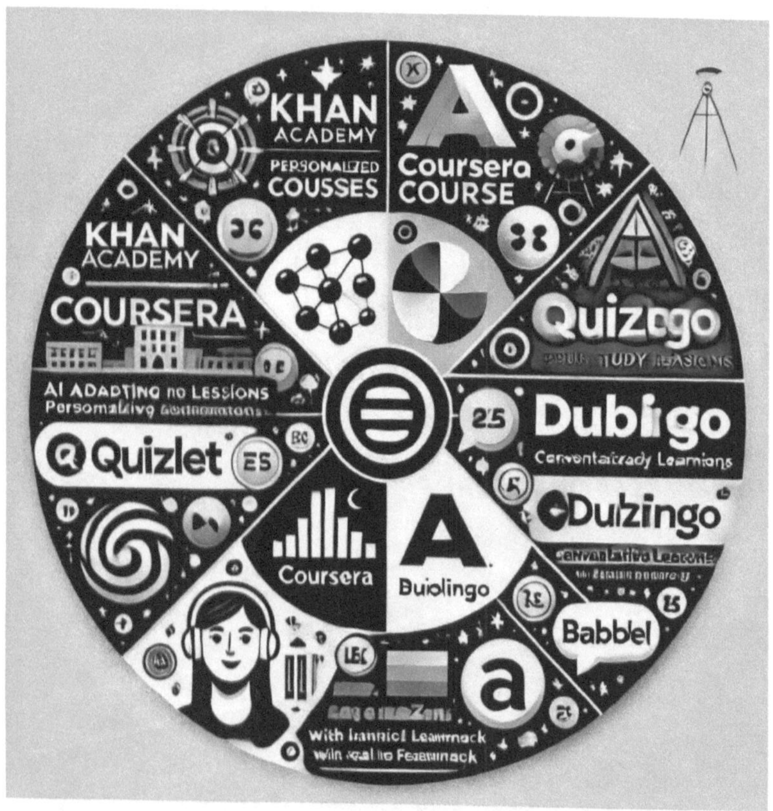

Khan Academy

Uses AI to adapt content and recommend lessons based on the student's progress and needs.

Coursera

Employs AI to provide personalized course recommendations and learning analytics.

Quizlet

Offers AI-generated study guides, flashcards, and quizzes tailored to individual learning styles.

Language Learning Assistants

Duolingo

An AI-driven language learning platform that adapts to your pace and tracks your progress.

Babbel

Combines AI with linguistic expertise to customize language lessons.

Mondly

Uses AI for conversational learning with speech recognition and real-time feedback.

STEM-Specific AI Tutors

Photomath

An app that uses AI to break down and explain solutions for math problems step by step.

ALEKS (Assessment and Learning in Knowledge Spaces)

Provides adaptive learning for math and science, adjusting questions based on student responses.

Carnegie Learning MATHia

AI-powered software designed to enhance math skills through step-by-step problem-solving.

Coding and Technology Platforms

Codeacademy

Offers AI-guided coding exercises and projects to improve programming skills.

Codio

An AI-based tool for teaching and assessing computer science concepts.

Grasshopper (by Google)

A beginner-friendly platform for learning coding basics with AI-powered feedback.

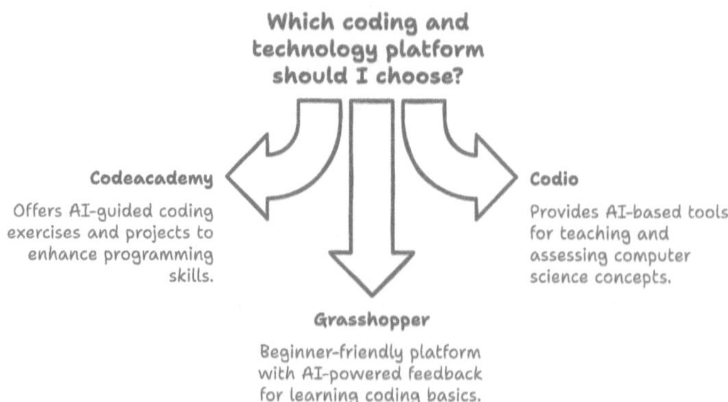

Conversational AI Tutors

Socratic (by Google)

An AI tutor app that answers questions across various subjects using conversational methods.

Replika

While primarily a chatbot, it helps users learn conversational skills and emotional intelligence.

ChatGPT (OpenAI)

Offers interactive learning experiences, explaining complex topics, helping with assignments, and fostering critical thinking.

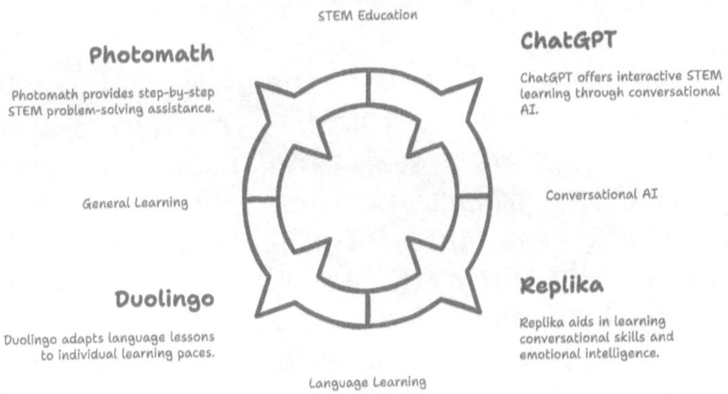

Revolutionising Conventional Classrooms

Incorporating these technological tools is converting conventional classrooms into technology-enhanced learning environments. Classrooms are evolving into collaborative and interactive environments that enable students to engage with the curriculum innovatively.

Educators may now integrate conventional teaching methods with technology, establishing a hybrid learning environment that fosters critical thinking, creativity, and problem-solving abilities. By utilising these technologies, educators can promote a more student-centred methodology in which learners engage actively in their education.

The Priority

The emergence of gamification, virtual reality simulations, and artificial intelligence-driven instructors signifies a substantial transformation in the educational framework. These technologies do not merely augment the learning experience; they fundamentally alter it. As education progresses, adopting these innovative tools will equip students to face future difficulties. By converting conventional classrooms into technology-enhanced learning environments, educators may cultivate a more engaging, individualised, and efficient educational experience for all students.

ᐁᐁᐁ

NINE

Implementing Education 5.0

"Education 5.0 promotes inclusivity, ensuring every learner has access to the tools and opportunities they need to thrive in a rapidly changing world."
– Dr. Linda Darling-Hammond, President of the Learning Policy Institute

Executing Education 5.0

Education 5.0 signifies a revolutionary paradigm in learning that amalgamates cutting-edge technologies, individualised education, and an emphasis on cultivating future-oriented abilities. The following are the measures for educational institutions, educators, and policymakers to implement Education 5.0 while addressing obstacles such as digital disparities, opposition to transformation, and prospective remedies.

Practical Measures for Educational Institutions

Incorporate Technology into Curriculum: Educational institutions should integrate AI, VR, AR, and other emerging technologies into their curricula to augment learning experiences. This can be accomplished through collaborations with technology firms and educational institutions.

Customised Learning Plans: Formulate tailored learning plans that address every learner's distinct requirements and interests. Employ data analytics to monitor progress and adjust instructional strategies accordingly.

Professional Development for Educators: Facilitate continuous training for teachers to give them the competencies required to apply new technology and pedagogical approaches effectively.

Collaborative Learning Environments: Cultivate a culture of cooperation among students via project-based learning and group activities that promote teamwork and critical analysis.

Community Engagement: Engage parents and the community in the educational process by organising workshops and informational sessions about the advantages of Education 5.0.

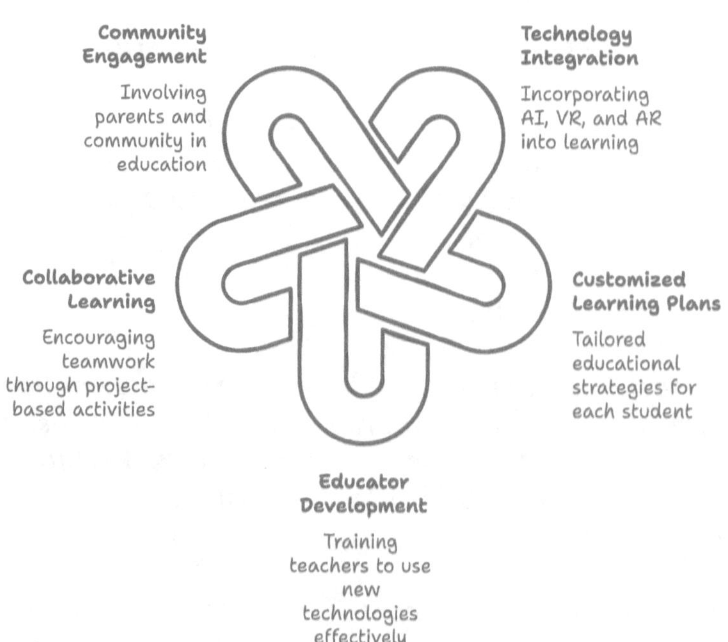

Practical Measures for Educators

Commit to Lifelong Learning: Educators must engage in ongoing professional development to remain informed about the latest educational technologies and pedagogical methodologies.

Employ Blended Learning Models: Integrate conventional pedagogical techniques with digital resources to establish a more adaptable and stimulating educational atmosphere.

Foster Student Agency: Students can select projects, establish objectives, and evaluate their progress. This will enable them to assume responsibility for their learning.

Integrate Practical Applications: Develop courses that link academic material to real-world challenges, motivating students to utilise their knowledge in tangible contexts.

Encourage a Growth Mindset: Cultivate resilience and flexibility in pupils by urging them to perceive setbacks as opportunities for development.

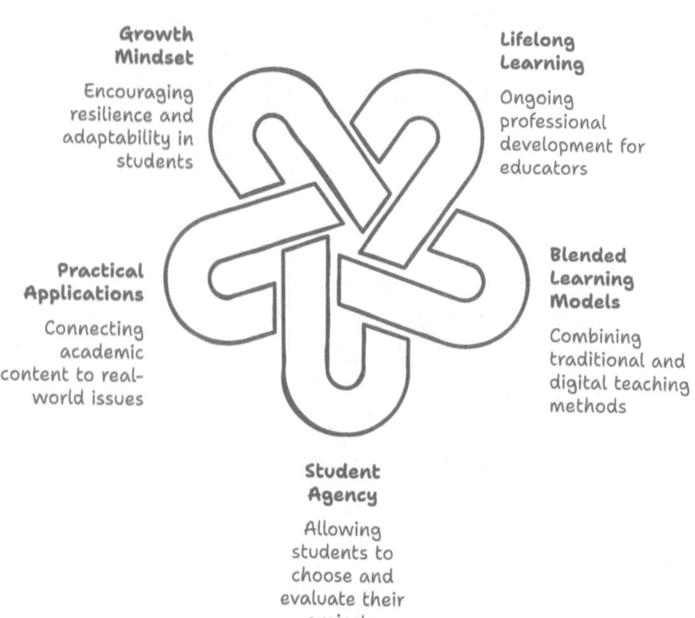

Enhancing Educational Practices
Growth Mindset
Encouraging resilience and adaptability in students
Lifelong Learning
Ongoing professional development for educators
Practical Applications
Connecting academic content to real-world issues
Blended Learning Models
Combining traditional and digital teaching methods
Student Agency
Allowing students to choose and evaluate their projects

ROLE OF TEACHERS IN EDUCATION 5.0

1. Customized Learning Paths
2. Active Engagement and Participation
3. Shift from Sage on the Stage to Guide on the Side
4. Promotion of Critical Thinking and Problem-Solving

Practical Measures for Policymakers

Invest in Infrastructure: Allocate financial resources to enhance digital infrastructure in educational institutions, guaranteeing that all students have access to essential technologies and resources.

Formulate Inclusive Policies: Establish policies that tackle the digital gap, guaranteeing fair access to technology for all pupils, irrespective of socioeconomic status.

Promote Research and Innovation: Finance research projects investigating novel educational technology and approaches, fostering innovation within the education sector.

Promote Collaboration: Foster alliances among

schools, corporations, and higher education institutions to establish a unified ecosystem that advances Education 5.0.

Monitor and Evaluate: Develop measures to evaluate the efficacy of Education 5.0 activities, facilitating ongoing enhancement and adjustment of tactics.

Obstacles and Resolutions

Digital Disparity

The digital divide constitutes a substantial obstacle, as numerous students lack access to technology and the internet.

Solution: Policymakers must prioritise financial support for technology in marginalised regions and establish community initiatives that supply students with devices and internet connectivity.

Opposition to Transformation

Challenge: Educators and institutions may resist embracing new approaches due to apprehension of the unfamiliar or insufficient comprehension.

Solution: To foster acceptance, offer extensive training and support for educators, emphasising successful case studies and the advantages of Education 5.0.

Curriculum Reform

Challenge: Revising curricula to conform to Education 5.0 concepts can be arduous and labour-intensive.

Solution: Execute incremental modifications, permitting pilot initiatives to be assessed and improved before a comprehensive implementation.

Evaluation Techniques

The challenge is that conventional evaluation methods

may inadequately evaluate the skills and competencies prioritised in Education 5.0.

Solution: Formulate new assessment methodologies that accurately represent student learning and development, including portfolios and performance-based evaluations.

Implementing Education 5.0 requires collaborative efforts among educational institutions, educators, and policymakers to adopt innovative technology and approaches. By tackling issues like the digital gap and opposition to change and implementing concrete measures, we can establish a more equal and efficient educational environment that equips students for the future.

ᐅᐅᐅ

TEN

CASE STUDIES AND SUCCESS STORIES

"Education 5.0 is about leveraging technology to amplify human potential, building a future where learners and machines co-create solutions for a better society."
– Dr. Alec Couros, Professor of Educational Technology

Institutional Achievement:

A prominent worldwide university used AI-driven personalised learning technologies, which increased student engagement by 30% and enhanced academic performance.

Innovative Classrooms:

A *Japanese high school incorporated virtual reality and the Internet of Things into its science curriculum, enabling pupils to perform virtual laboratory experiments and enhancing their interest in STEM disciplines.*

A rural school in India implemented gamification in language education, which significantly increased literacy rates among disadvantaged youngsters.

African non-profit organisations collaborated with local enterprises to synchronise vocational training with industry requirements, establishing a sustainable employment pipeline.

Each case study illustrates the transformative potential of Education 5.0 principles on individuals and communities, motivating widespread implementation.

My Experiential visits to Finland/ Hongkong, and China came up with the following inputs:

Finland

Finland's Education 5.0 is a masterclass in personalized learning and technological integration. Schools use AI and robotics to tailor experiences while prioritizing emotional intelligence and creativity. The

Finnish approach balances technology and pedagogy, ensuring students engage in problem-solving and hands-on learning, making education both future-focused and deeply human-centred.

Teach Like Finland

Hong Kong

Hong Kong's Education 5.0 is a vibrant blend of cutting-edge technology and experiential learning. Schools emphasize STEM, with AI and robotics driving innovation in classrooms. This integration equips students with critical thinking and adaptability, fostering a future-ready mindset in one of the world's most fast-paced and tech-driven regions.

Japan

Japan's implementation of Education 5.0 harmonizes robotics, AI, and traditional values. Students engage in experiential, hands-on learning while cultivating teamwork and discipline. The curriculum aligns seamlessly with industry demands, preparing students for an AI-driven future while preserving Japan's cultural emphasis on respect, perseverance, and holistic development.

Education in Japan: Insights and Reflections from My Visit

♥♥♥

,,

ELEVEN

FUTURE OF EDUCATION 5.0

"In the world of Education 5.0, empathy and technology are not opposites but partners in crafting a compassionate and innovative learning experience."
– Dr. Pasi Sahlberg, Finnish Educator and Author

Prospects of Education 5.0

The future of education is set for significant transformation as we proceed towards Education 5.0, which will mark the incorporation of cutting-edge technologies and novel teaching methodologies. This document examines projected educational changes, such as the emergence of AI-driven teaching assistants and the formation of worldwide learning networks. Furthermore, it conjectures the progression towards Education 6.0, anticipating a more integrated and individualised learning experience.

Artificial Intelligence-Driven Teaching Assistants

A prominent trend in Education 5.0 is integrating artificial intelligence into the educational setting. AI-driven teaching assistants are anticipated to enhance personalised learning experiences significantly. These intelligent systems may evaluate individual student performance, modify instructional materials, and deliver real-time feedback, enabling educators to concentrate on more intricate teaching responsibilities. Using AI, educational institutions may augment student engagement and enhance learning outcomes.

International Educational Networks

As technology progressively dismantles geographical barriers, global learning networks are essential to Education 5.0. These networks link students and educators from varied backgrounds, promoting collaboration and cultural exchange. Online platforms enable learners to access extensive resources, participate in virtual classrooms, and engage in international initiatives. This interconnection enhances the educational experience and equips students with a global workforce.

Advancement Towards Education 6.0

The impending shift from Education 5.0 to Education 6.0 is anticipated to transform the educational environment significantly. Education 6.0 will likely prioritise comprehensive development by incorporating emotional intelligence, creativity, and critical thinking into the curriculum. The function of educators will transition from conventional lecturers to facilitators of learning, assisting students in interpreting intricate knowledge and cultivating a development attitude.

Furthermore, incorporating immersive technologies like virtual reality (VR) and augmented reality (AR) will establish dynamic learning environments that replicate real-world experiences. This experiential learning methodology will increase student engagement and retention, rendering education more pertinent and significant.

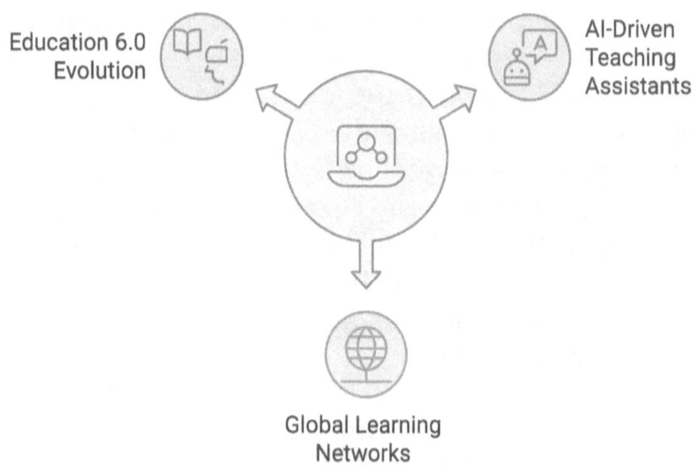

"With Education 5.0, the goal is not just to teach students how to adapt but to empower them to lead the change."
– Dr. Tony Wagner, Senior Research Fellow, Learning Policy Institute

The future of education is promising, as Education 5.0 facilitates creative methodologies and technologies that improve learning experiences. As we foresee the transition to Education 6.0, we must adopt these changes and prepare ourselves for a more individualised, integrated, and comprehensive educational paradigm. Utilising AI, promoting international cooperation, and emphasising holistic skill development can establish an academic framework that addresses the requirements of future generations.

❦❦❦

TWELVE

25 Paths to Implementing Education 5.0

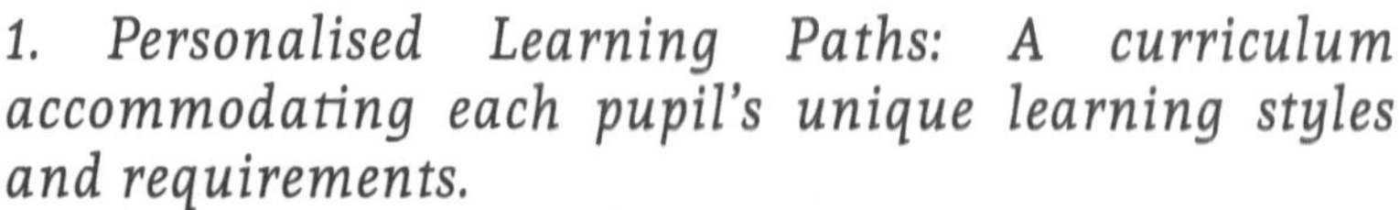

1. *Personalised Learning Paths: A curriculum accommodating each pupil's unique learning styles and requirements.*

2. *Competency-Based Education: Prioritises the acquisition of skills and knowledge throughout classroom time.*

3. *AI Integration in Education: Using AI tools to evaluate pupil progress and offer immediate feedback.*

4. *Immersive Technologies: The utilisation of AR/VR to facilitate experiential learning in disciplines such as science, history, and geography.*

5. *The STEAM Focus is the comprehensive integration of science, technology, engineering, arts, and*

mathematics to provide a thorough education.

6. Collaborative Learning Platforms: Instruments that promote communication and teamwork through shared initiatives and group activities.

7. Digital Citizenship Education involves instructing students on how to use technology and navigate the digital realm responsibly.

8. Ethics and Emotional Intelligence (EQ): Curriculum intended to cultivate social skills, self-awareness, and empathy.

9. Teaching the significance of sustainable development and promoting eco-conscious practices: Sustainability Education.

10. Cultural Understanding and Global Competence: Promoting cultural comprehension and raising awareness of global concerns.

11. AI-Driven Assessments: Adaptive assessment mechanisms in accordance with each student's progress and competency levels.

12. Real-World Problem Solving: Activities and projects designed to address real-world challenges.

13. Flexible Learning Spaces: Classrooms specifically designed to facilitate interactive and dynamic learning experiences.

14. Cross-Curricular Integration: Integrating concepts from various subjects to demonstrate their interconnectedness.

15. Emphasise Creativity and Innovation: Motivating students to think creatively and innovate across disciplines.

16. Coding and Computational Thinking: The introduction of coding as a fundamental skill for problem-solving.

17. Teacher Training for Digital Tools: Educators undergo consistent professional development to remain informed about technological advancements.

18. AI-Powered Virtual Assistants: These are assistive technologies that facilitate the completion of daily duties for both students and educators.

19. Data-Driven Insights: Utilising analytics to enhance instruction strategies and monitor student performance.

20. Project-based learning (PBL) involves hands-on initiatives that foster critical thinking and the application of knowledge.

21. Parental Engagement in Education: Facilitating real-time updates and collaboration with parents through technology platforms.

22. Lifelong Learning Mindset: Encouraging students to maintain a mindset of continuous learning and adaptability.

23. Integration of Local and Global Cultures:

Highlighting the importance of respect and appreciation for cultural diversity.

24. Hybrid Learning Models: The seamless integration of online and in-class learning environments.

25. Emphasise Holistic Development: Achieving comprehensive development by balancing academics, sports, the arts, and mental well-being.

The collective objective of these attributes is to establish a school ecosystem that is prepared for the future and encourages lifelong learning, adaptability, and innovation.

❧❧❧

THIRTEEN

10 "Do-Nots" for the Implementation of Education 5.0 in Schools

To guarantee its efficacy, Education 5.0 necessitates meticulous planning and execution. To maintain alignment with its objectives, it is crucial to steer clear of these prevalent pitfalls:

#1 Teacher training should not be neglected.

For what reason? To adjust to new technologies and methodologies, educators require appropriate training. Ineffective implementation may result from neglecting professional development.

#2 Failure to prioritise infrastructure

For what reason? The absence of adequate technology infrastructure, including reliable internet, AR/VR devices, and smart classrooms, can impede the efficacy of education. 5.0.

#3 Excluding All Stakeholders

Why? Ignoring the input of instructors, students, and parents can result in resistance to and a decrease in adopting new practices.

#4 Failure to cater to the requirements of students

For what reason? A one-size-fits-all approach undermines the personalisation aspect of Education

5.0, leaving some pupils behind.

#5 Neglecting ethical considerations

For what reason? Neglecting the ethical application of technology can result in cyberbullying, data privacy concerns, and misconduct.

#6 Failure to incorporate soft skills

For what reason? Holistic development is prioritised in Education 5.0. Incomplete education can result from disregarding empathy, creativity, and collaboration skills.

#7 Failure to Address the Digital Divide

For what reason? Economically disadvantaged students may be denied the opportunity to ultimately benefit from technology and resources if they are not provided with equitable access.

#8 Failure to monitor progress

For what reason? Schools cannot quantify the impact or pinpoint areas for improvement without consistent assessment and feedback.

#9 Failure to Maintain a Balance Between Human Interaction and Technology

Why? Excessive reliance on technology can diminish the importance of human connection, essential for emotional and social development.

#10 The school's vision is not being met.

For what reason? Creating confusion and a lack of direction can result from implementing Education 5.0 without fully aligning it with the school's mission and objectives.

ᔕᔕᔕ

About The Author

Dr Dheeraj Mehrotra is a distinguished educational leader and innovator with over three decades of experience transforming education through excellence and innovation. A recipient of the President of India's National Teacher Award (2006), he is a certified expert in Six Sigma (White and Yellow Belt), Neuro-Linguistic Programming (NLP), and Total Quality Management (TQM). His specialisation encompasses Academic Audits, School Quality Assurance and Accreditation (SQAA), and the implementation of Kaizen and 5S in schools. As an accomplished author, Dr Mehrotra has published over 200 books on various topics, including computer science, artificial intelligence, digital body language, quality circles, and school management. His contributions also include developing over 150 free educational mobile apps for teachers, students, and parents, a feat recognised by the Limca

Book of Records and the India Book of Records. Dr Mehrotra has served as Principal at prestigious institutions such as De Indian Public School in New Delhi, NPS International School in Guwahati, and Kunwar's Global School in Lucknow. He has also served as Education Officer at GEMS in Gurgaon, making significant contributions to the global education community. As a premium UDEMY instructor, Dr Mehrotra has created over 500 courses that have impacted more than 800,000 learners across 180 countries. Additionally, as the founder and president of the IoT Society of India, he champions the integration of technology in education globally.

References: Further Reading

Education 5.0: The Future of Learning

AI in Schools Transforming Education

Digital Leadership in Schools: Shaping the Future